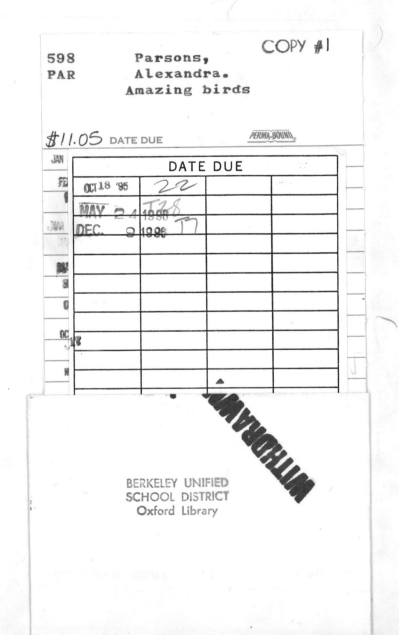

Amazing
Birds

Amazing
Birds

WRITTEN BY
ALEXANDRA PARSONS

PHOTOGRAPHED BY
JERRY YOUNG

ALFRED A. KNOPF • NEW YORK

Editor Scott Steedman
Designers Ann Cannings and Margo Beamish-White
Senior art editor Jacquie Gulliver
Editorial director Sue Unstead
Art director Anne-Marie Bulat

Special photography by Jerry Young
Illustrations by Mark Iley and John Bendall
Animals supplied by Trevor Smith's Animal World
Editorial consultants
The staff of the Natural History Museum, London

This is a Borzoi Book published by Alfred A. Knopf, Inc.

This Eyewitness Junior Book has been conceived, edited, and
designed by Dorling Kindersley Limited

First American edition, 1990

Manufactured in Italy   0 9 8 7 6 5 4 3 2 1

Library of Congress Cataloging in Publication Data
Parsons, Alexandra
Amazing birds / written by Alexandra Parsons;
photographs by Jerry Young.
p. cm. — (Eyewitness juniors)
Summary: Text and photographs describe amazing members of the
bird world, including the vulture, flamingo, and hummingbird.
1. Birds — Juvenile literature. [1. Birds.] I. Young, Jerry, ill.
II. Title. III. Series: Parsons, Alexandra. Eyewitness juniors.
QL676.2.P38 1990   598 — dc20   89-38943
ISBN 0-679-80223-1
ISBN 0-679-90223-6 (lib. bdg.)

Color reproduction by Colourscan, Singapore
Typeset by Windsorgraphics, Ringwood, Hampshire
Printed in Italy by A. Mondadori Editore, Verona

Contents

What is a bird?

There are 9,000 different kinds of bird – birds that sing and birds that squawk, pretty birds and plain ones, huge birds and tiny ones, birds that soar high in the sky and birds that cannot fly at all.

Flap flop

Humans have always wanted to fly like the birds. The first people to build flying machines copied bird wings and tried to flap with their arms. But the human body is just not made for flying.

Looking back

Most birds, especially owls, have good eyesight. Owls can swivel their heads nearly all the way around to see in every direction.

The silent hunter

Owls hunt at night, when most other birds are asleep. They take mice and other small animals by surprise because they fly so quietly.

What have they got?

All birds have two legs, two wings, a beak, and hundreds of feathers. And all birds lay eggs.

Pointy toes

Most birds have four toes. Birds that perch on small branches have three toes pointing forward, and birds that climb trees have two pointing forward and two pointing back. Water birds have webs between their toes.

percher   *climber*   *paddle*

An owl's "ears" are actually tufts of feathers.

Eagle owl
This rare bird is the largest owl of all. It may not look very fierce, but it can kill and eat a small fox.

Feathers
Birds have three kinds of feathers. Flight feathers in their wings and tails help them to fly, and downy feathers keep them warm. Body feathers cover the rest of their bodies.

flight feathers

Barn owl
This little owl roosts and makes its nest in barns and old buildings. It couldn't tackle anything much larger than a field mouse.

downy feathers

The eagle owl has huge claws, or talons.

body feathers

9

The flamingo

This remarkable bird has long legs, a long neck, and a beak that acts like a huge sieve. It lives around salty lakes and rivers in the warm parts of the world, from Africa to the Caribbean.

Sift and sieve

The flamingo's upper bill has little sieves on each side. To eat, the bird takes in a beakful of water, then uses its lower bill to pump the water out through the sieves. Only the tiniest pieces of food are left behind.

Daily milk

Just like a human baby, a flamingo chick lives on a kind of milk. Both parents dribble a bright red liquid from their beaks when the hungry baby starts to squawk.

Togetherness

Flamingos like to stick together. Sometimes they live in flocks of over a million birds.

Mud pies

A flamingo nest is not much to look at. The male and female build it together, using their beaks to push blobs of mud into a big pile.

Heads down

To eat, flamingos poke their heads into the water upside down. Some feed on tiny plants, called algae, which float in the water. Others prefer to trawl the mud for shrimps.

Why is the flamingo pink?

Because of the food it eats. Pink coloring in algae and shrimps passes into the bird's body and comes out in its feathers.

Party treat

A long time ago, in ancient Rome, pickled flamingo tongues were considered a special treat. At feasts they were served on gold dishes.

To make feeding easier, a flamingo's knees bend backward – unlike yours.

Some flamingos are pinker than others, but they all have a few black feathers in their wings.

The lesser flamingo

There are six different kinds of flamingo. This one, found in Africa, is called the lesser flamingo.

Parrots

There are more than 300 kinds of parrot, the most colorful of all birds. Many live in tropical forests, high up among the trees. Others live in open bush country.

Fluffy face
Many parrots fluff up the feathers on their heads when they are excited or angry.

When a bird flaps its wings, the long feathers at the tips lift it into the air.

Singsong
Most parrots do not sing on their own – they just squawk loudly. But some will sing any song that you teach them.

The kakapo
This rare New Zealand parrot cannot fly. Instead, it hops around the forest floor at night.

Jet set
The little Alexandrine parakeet, a type of parrot, is a very fast flier. It is found in the jungles of Thailand in Southeast Asia.

retty parrot

his parrot is called the green-
inged macaw. It comes from
outh America. Macaws are
opular pets because they
ke a lot of attention
d can be taught to
nitate human
ices. They
ay live for
er 30 years.

Heave-ho
Some parrots'
beaks are so strong
they can use them to
haul themselves up trees.

nut eater   *insect eater*

Beaks to order
Birds' beaks help
them catch their favorite
food. Nuts and seeds crack
in a parrot's short, strong beak.
Insects are snapped up in a long,
thin bill. Slippery fish are gripped
firmly in a saw-edged beak.

fish eater

Hold on tight
Birds have to sleep without falling off
their perches. They have a long, string-
like tendon attached to each toe. While
they sleep, this tendon locks
the toes around the branch.

tendons

13

The pelican

This unusual bird looks clumsy waddling on land with its big body, stubby legs, and webbed feet. It is a water bird, able to fly, glide, swim, and catch fish in its built-in fishing net.

Swoop and scoop
The pouch on a pelican's beak can stretch very wide. A brown pelican can plunge into the water and scoop up fish in its beak like a fisherman with a net.

Leaky beak
The pelican scoops up a lot of water as it fishes. It has to spill the water out of its beak before taking off – otherwise the bird would be too heavy to fly!

Bare babies
Baby pelicans hatch from their eggs without any feathers at all. But within three days they are covered in soft, brown down.

A lot of lunch

Full-grown pelicans eat an awful lot. They can gobble up as much as 11 pounds of fish a day – that is the same as 20 school lunches!

Water birds' feathers are coated with a special oil so that the water slides right off them.

Holiday time

In the autumn, many birds fly someplace warm where there is lots to eat. The Dalmatian pelican (left) leaves Yugoslavia to spend the winter by the Nile River in Egypt.

Open wide!

When the mother pelican has a beak full of fish, she flies back to the nest to feed her chicks. The chicks stick their heads into her pouch and eat their fill.

The vulture

Vultures are nature's garbage collectors. They feed on dead bodies, eating everything except the bones.

Sunbathing

Like all birds, vultures hav oils in their feathers to kee them clean. After a meal, the birds sit with their win spread to soak up the sunlight, which keeps the oils in good shape

Feeling peckish?

This is a hooded vulture from Africa. It sits in the trees, watching and waiting for other animals to die.

Vultures have very powerful, curved beaks for ripping flesh off bones.

Rare bird

The Californian condor is a member of the vulture family. It is one of the largest and rarest birds in the world.

In for the kill

Vultures gather quickly around a dying animal. As soon as one bird goes for the corpse, the whole flock will come rushing down. They can pick an antelope's bones clean in 20 minutes.

Blush pink

This fierce-looking bird actually blushes! At least, that's what it looks like. When a vulture is angry or excited, the bare skin around its face turns pink.

Cancel the concert

You won't get much of a song from vultures. They just hiss and grunt in a nasty way.

The penguin

These smartly dressed black-and-white birds live among the icebergs in the cold Antarctic Ocean. Penguins are water birds that cannot fly. But they can swim very well, using their wings as flippers to "fly" through the water.

Thanks, Dad!
Keeping an egg warm on the ice is a difficult business. The father emperor penguin balances the egg on his feet, tucked under a cozy flap of skin.

Well caught!
Penguins catch all their food underwater. They can move very fast, and their spiky tongues help them to grip slippery fish in their beaks.

Welcome home, dear!
After the mother emperor penguin has laid the egg, she waddles off to sea for a long feed. Father penguin has to shuffle around for two whole months with his baby on his feet, unable to get to the sea and catch fish. He must be very pleased to see the mother penguin when she returns.

Tobogganing
The best way to get around on snow and ice is to slide. That is what penguins do, using their fat bellies as toboggans.

Nursery school
When baby penguins have grown large enough, they gather together for safety while their parents go fishing. A few adult birds stay around to guard the youngsters.

The penguin has a thick blanket of fat under its skin for warmth.

Flat feet
The penguin uses its big webbed feet like the rudder of a boat, to steer itself in the water.

Waterproof suit
penguin's body is overed with three yers of tiny, water-roof feathers, to keep warm and dry in and ut of the water.

Good swimmer
A penguin is an odd shape for a bird – it looks more like a seal. Its sleek body is perfect for diving and swimming. This fine fellow is a Humboldt penguin.

The swan

The graceful swan is one of the largest water birds. It glides along lakes and slow-moving rivers, feeding on grass and water weeds.

A swan has 25,000 feathers more than any other bird.

Fairy tale swans

There is a Danish fairy tale about a whole family of princes who are turned into swans. They have to fly off and fetch their sister to help break the spell.

Built-in paddles

Swans have big webbed feet to help them paddle along in the water and waddle around on the shore.

A warm nest

Once a year the mute swan builds a huge nest out of grass and reeds. The female lays five to eight eggs in the nest.

Hitching a ride
Young swans are called cygnets (SIG-nits). They often ride around on their mother's back.

Black magic
Black swans come from Australia. Like all swans, the male and female are very faithful to each other. They will stay together for years, caring for their babies and teaching them to fly and swim.

A honk or a whistle?
The mute swan (left) honks now and then. Most swans whistle.

Ugly duckling
Cygnets are a dull gray color and are a bit clumsy. Their feathers don't turn white until they are about three years old.

The peacock

The male peacock has a fabulous fan. He uses it to court the duller-looking female, or peahen.

Rear view
The peacock's fan is not a tail. It is made of back feathers and is called a train. The bird's real tail holds the train up.

Backward shuffle
The peacock opens his fan only when he is trying to charm a peahen. First he backs up to her. Then he spins suddenly to face her and dazzle her with his beautiful, quivering train.

Alarm call
Both the peacock and the peahen have good eyesight and hearing, so they are quick to sense danger. When they feel threatened, they give an incredibly loud shriek. This noise often warns other birds and animals in the forest.

Hypnotic eyes

The shimmering "eyes" on the peacock's train are a beautiful sight. They certainly fascinate the peahen – she may even be hypnotized by them.

Tail of love

The male lyrebird of Australia has a tail for attracting females too. It looks just like a lyre, a harp played in Greece long ago.

Look at me!

"As vain as a peacock" – that's what we call people who strut around in fancy clothes with their nose in the air.

A peacock's train can be 6 feet high – taller than an average human.

On the run

You might think a peacock would trip over his long train, but he doesn't. With the feathers trailing behind him, he can run through the forest quickly and quietly.

The ostrich

The biggest birds in the world can't fly at all. But they can certainly run. The African ostrich can zip along at 45 miles per hour, which is faster than the fastest sprinter.

A real rhea
The rhea (REE-uh; right) is an ostrich-like bird that lives in South America.

Shoulder high
A tall man standing next to an ostrich will only come up to the bird's shoulders.

What a dish!
Imagine eating an ostrich egg! One egg is bigger than a grapefruit and as heavy as 4,500 hummingbird eggs.

South American feather duster
Like the ostrich, the rhea has beautiful, soft feathers. In South America they are used to make feather dusters.

On the move
Ostriches roam the grassy plains of Africa in groups. They often join herds of antelope or cattle.

Bugs and greens
The rhea eats leaves, grass, and insects. The bird spots food easily with its huge eyes and snaps it up in its large, flat beak.

Fashionable bird
Ostrich feathers are much admired and were once used to decorate hats and dresses. The cream-colored shells of ostrich eggs were even made into table decorations.

Walking on cushions
The African ostrich is the only bird that has just two toes. Each toe has a soft pad like a cushion underneath it, to stop the heavy ostrich from sinking into the soft sand.

Egg sit
The male rhea makes eggs with as many as 12 different females. All of the females lay their green or yellow eggs in the same nest, where the male sits on the eggs himself.

The hummingbird

The hummingbird is the smallest bird in the world. It eats tiny insects and sucks nectar from flowers like a bee.

A hummingbird can flap its wings 80 times a second.

A hummingbird's feathers are iridescent, which means they change color in the light.

Feeding and flapping

Hummingbirds hover while they feed, flapping so fast that all you can see is a blur of wings. They use up so much energy that they have to keep feeding to give them the energy to keep flapping.

Sipping through a straw

A hummingbird's tongue is like a long thin tube that sticks out from the end of its beak. It uses this special tongue like a straw, to suck nectar from flowers.

Soft and cozy

The hummingbird builds its nest from thistledown, lichen, and spiders' web

Teeny tiny eggs

The world's smallest bird also lays the world's smallest eggs. It always lays two, each one the size of your little fingernail.

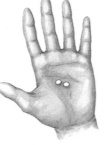

Flying champion

Three cheers for the hummingbird! It is the only bird in the world that can fly sideways and backward.

Weak feet

Hummingbirds can't really walk. They have weak little feet that are perfect for perching but hopeless for hiking.

Hummmmm

The hummingbird gets its name from the whirring sound its wings make.

Glittering feathers

There are over 300 different kinds of hummingbird, and all of them have brilliant blue, green, or purple feathers. Some hummingbirds have extremely long beaks for reaching deep into flowers.

How birds fly

Birds fly in three ways: gliding, flapping, or hovering. Different birds use different kinds of flight, depending on where they live and how they feed.

Big sea birds like this albatross can glide without flapping for hours. Sometimes they don't land for weeks!

Gliding
This looks easy! When birds glide they hold their wings out stiffly and are kept up by the air rushing under and over their wings. But they have to flap every now and then – or find a puff of wind to lift them up or carry them forward.

Flapping
All birds flap. Flapping helps the bird to take off or climb higher in the air.

First the bird pushes down with its wings to lift it up and carry it forward.

Then it draws its wings up again, ready for another push down.

Hovering

Most birds cannot hover for long. It means flapping the wings so fast that the bird stays up in the air without moving – it just hangs there! Hummingbirds, terns, and kestrels are the best hoverers.

Kestrel

The kestrel (above) is a kind of falcon. It is a very skillful flier and swoops down on mice and birds and carries them off in its talons.

Index